JUDICAELLE CELESTIN

# What Happens When Women Fully Surrender and Follow God's Calling?

*Learning to Say Yes to God After Deep Pain and Disappointment*

*Copyright © 2025 by Judicaelle Celestin*

*All rights reserved. No part of this publication may be reproduced, stored or transmitted in any form or by any means, electronic, mechanical, photocopying, recording, scanning, or otherwise without written permission from the publisher. It is illegal to copy this book, post it to a website, or distribute it by any other means without permission.*

*First edition*

*This book was professionally typeset on Reedsy. Find out more at reedsy.com*

# Contents

1 Introduction   1
2 Recognizing God's Call   14
3 Becoming Rooted—Laying a Spiritual Foundation   28
4 Walking in Purpose—Discovering and Using Your Gifts   37
5 A woman of God does not just say "yes" once; she lives a...   46
6 One Last Request: Share Your Yes   57

# 1

## Introduction

### The Power of Saying Yes to God

What if the most powerful thing you could ever say did not have to be loud or fancy? What if it was said in a quiet moment between you and God with just one simple word: **Yes.**

This book is not just about saying yes. It is about what happens when a woman truly gives her yes to God from the heart. Not because she is perfect. Not because she has it all figured out. But because she is willing to trust Him.

**The Power of Saying Yes to God** is for any woman who is ready to stop holding back and start living with real purpose. Maybe you have felt God speaking to your heart but were not sure what to do next. Maybe fear or doubt is holding you back. This book can help.

This book is filled with stories from the Bible, real-life examples, questions to help you think deeper, and simple steps to build your faith. You will learn how to move forward even when you feel afraid, how to grow closer to God, and how to walk boldly into the life He created just for you.

**Inside, you'll discover**

- Ways to let go of your fears and worries and follow God's path, even when it feels small or scary
- How to hear God's voice in your everyday life
- Why obeying God leads to growth and opens new doors
- How fear, insecurity, and distractions try to hold you back
- How prayer, scripture, and community can strengthen your faith
- What happens when you finally say "yes" to God and how it changes everything

But most of all, I want you to know this: your yes matters. Even if it feels small. Even if it feels scary, God can do something amazing with it.

## 1. Why This Topic Matters

Right now, a lot of women feel stressed and overwhelmed. Life is busy and noisy. There are so many people telling you what you should do and how you should live. It can make you feel like you are not doing enough, not good enough, or like you are falling behind. You might even feel like something is missing, like you do not know your real purpose.

That is why this message matters. God is still calling women today. He is still talking to us, guiding us, and asking us to trust

INTRODUCTION

Him. He wants you to stand strong in your faith, follow His truth, and live the life He made just for you.

Saying yes to God does not mean you have to do something huge. It means trusting Him with your whole life, right where you are. It means choosing to follow Him even when you are scared. It means knowing that God can do amazing things with your yes more than you could ever do on your own.

You do not have to wait until life is perfect to say yes. God wants your yes now. This book is not just here to make you feel good it is here to help you. Inside, you will find helpful tips, real encouragement, and powerful truths to help you grow in your faith and take the next step.

## 2. My Story and Why I Wrote This Book

I did not write this book because I know everything. I wrote it because I have been through a lot and asked hard questions. There were times when I felt confused, hurt, and unsure of what God wanted from me. I have asked, "Is God really calling me?" and "Can someone like me be used by Him?" I know what it is like to doubt, to feel not good enough, and to be afraid of the future. But things started to change when I said, "God, I do not have all the answers, but I trust You."

There is also a personal part of my story I want to share with you.

**Family issue:**

When I was young, around seven years old, something terrible almost happened to me. I almost get raped, but God saved me. My mom was not paying attention or protecting me the way she should have. Even at that young age, I began to understand life and how evil people can sometimes be. That moment was the first time I realized how alone and unsafe I truly felt at home.

Growing up was incredibly difficult for me because of the challenges my sister and I faced with our mother. Her behavior was unpredictable and often hurtful, leaving deep emotional wounds that shaped much of our early lives. We struggled with the way she treated us, the things she said, and the way she made us feel. It was not just occasional conflict; it was a constant battle to feel safe, heard, and loved in our own home.

Those experiences did not stay in the past. They followed us as we grew, influencing how we saw ourselves, how we trusted others, and how we navigated the world. The pain we carried was not always visible, but it was very real. Learning to heal from it has been a long and ongoing journey.

But through it all, my faith became a light in the darkness. Little by little, I began to heal—not overnight, but one prayer at a time. God showed me that my past does not define me. He gave me strength, purpose, and a reason to keep going. Now, I am not just starting to heal. I am growing. I am choosing to break the cycle, to live with hope, and to help others who feel broken too. My journey has not been easy, but it is shaping me into someone stronger, wiser, and full of grace.

**Learn about my mother's behavior and a short story when I was kid, teenager, and adult:**

My mother has always been very aggressive and controlling. Her need for control affected every part of my life, from the smallest decisions to the biggest moments. I remember when I was in high school, my mom would tell me exactly which street to walk on after school, just so she could meet me halfway and watch my every move. At first, I didn't have a problem with it because I understood that a mother wants to protect her children. But over time, as I grew up and began to see her

## INTRODUCTION

actions more clearly, I realized she was very controlling. The way she acted sometimes even scared me.

Yes, I always did what my mother told me. However, one day, my cousin and her friends warned me not to walk alone. They told me the street my mother had told me to take was dangerous. A young girl had recently been killed there by some bad people. They said I would be safer walking with them. Other people around us also warned me to listen to my cousin and avoid that street. I got scared and decided to walk with my cousin and her friends instead.

But my mom was waiting for me on the street she had told me to take. When she didn't see me there, she became very angry. I was only 13 years old at the time.

When I got home, my mother wasn't there yet. But when she arrived, she started yelling at me and slapped me across the face. Other people tried to stop her, shouting and trying to explain that I had avoided a dangerous street. But she didn't listen to anyone. She didn't even ask me why I had taken a different road. She beat me and screamed at me to kiss the floor, then told me to repeat after her: "I will never do this again."

Another hard part of growing up was not knowing who my real dad was. My mom always had different men in her life. This situation really hurt me. I am a quiet and shy person, so I never asked questions about my dad. She would bring men home whom she assumed were our fathers. Sometimes, she acted like they were not even our fathers. This made me feel very confused and lost. I never felt close to the man my mother brought home and called my father. He was a police officer, but he was very aggressive. He practiced voodoo and often performed rituals for people. When I lived with him for a few months, I saw him repeatedly hit his girlfriend in the stomach.

He once beat my mother too, hitting her in the stomach. I remember her stomach became very swollen afterward, and she had many injuries and bruises that left scars. She even accused me of being the reason she got beat up. I was probably around 10 or 12 years old at the time. One time, my mom even changed my name to his, just so he would pay for my schooling. But even after she changed my name, he did not want to pay. Thankfully, my cousin, a young man in our family, stepped up and paid for my school.

I remember feeling very confused when teachers and students started calling me by a different name. During exams, I would sometimes write my old name because that was what I was used to. One teacher got confused and asked me why I wrote a different name. She told me to use my real name. I felt embarrassed and didn't know what to do.

A few years later, when I started high school, my mom changed my name back. I was very happy to have my name back. Even though I still felt lost and confused at times, I learned something important: my real identity isn't in a name or in what people say about me. My identity is in what God says about me. He says I am chosen, loved, and that I belong to Him.

INTRODUCTION

Growing up, my sister and I were never close. I tried to have a good relationship with her, but it never worked. She would always put me down and make me feel like I was stupid or a slow person. One time, she even said, "You do not have any brain." I just stood there, not sure if I heard her right. My heart sank, and I felt my face get hot. I laughed a little, hoping it was a joke, but it was not. She meant it. Even now, she still treats me like I am a slow person.

I was eighteen years old when she said I did not have a brain. Even though we were sisters, we were never very close. We did not hang out much or talk like some sisters do. Still, I never thought she would say something like that to me. Her words hurt me deeply; not just because they were mean, but because they came from someone in my own family. If a stranger had said it, maybe I could have ignored it. But when it comes from your own sister, it is different. I felt like I did not matter. After my sister said that, I did not say much. I just stayed still. But inside, I wanted to cry. This kind of childhood left me with a lot of hurt and confusion.

Through all of this, I have always believed that I am a child of God. I began serving Him and accepting Him as my Savior around the age of 9 or 10. I spent most of my time going to church, school, and work. I never wanted to get involved in anything that went against my values. I have always tried to respect myself and do what is right. Sometimes people think that being nice means you are weak or not smart, but that is not true. I am a caring person and a young woman growing in God. I make mistakes, yes, but I am still learning.

Another one of the hardest and most heartbreaking moments in my life happened during my high school graduation. A day that was supposed to be filled with joy and celebration. My professors and advisors were so proud of me. After years of hard work and dedication, they were eager to meet my family.

INTRODUCTION

I was excited too and hopeful that, for once, I could share a happy moment with my mother and my sister. But when the ceremony ended and the crowd flooded the area, I could not find my mother anywhere. I searched through the crowd. I called her several times, hoping she'd answer, but the phone just kept ringing. My heart sank. I felt lost in a sea of student who were laughing, hugging, and taking pictures with their families while I stood there, alone.

When I could not find my mother, I called the taxi driver. He was a friend of my mother's who had brought her to the graduation ceremony. I told him that I called my mom, and she did not answer her phone. Seeing how overwhelmed and distressed I was, he gently suggested that I go sit somewhere quiet and try calling her again. I took his advice and began walking toward a nearby cafe to gather myself.

As I was walking, my phone rang, it was her. I quickly answered and told her that I had stepped away from the ceremony to a quieter spot. I asked her to meet me at the cafe. But instead of understanding, she exploded in anger over the phone. Her voice was loud, harsh, and filled with rage. I tried to stay calm, but tears almost welled up in my eyes. The tension was so obvious that a few parents and students nearby looked over and gently asked, "Are you okay?".

I wanted to say yes, but I wasn't. I was overwhelmed, embarrassed, and deeply hurt. A moment that was supposed to be filled with pride and joy had quickly turned into another painful event. When I finally saw her, she was with my sister. She was really angry because I had sat somewhere without asking her first. She said I had no right to leave the graduation ceremony or listen to the taxi driver's suggestion to go sit at the cafe. She started yelling at me and told me to get in the taxi.

Once we were in the car, she kept shouting and then she started hitting me in my head and all over. When I got home, she beat me more. It was a painful and scary moment that I will never forget. The next day, my mother told me to get dressed the same way so we could take a picture as if nothing had happened. This moment stayed with me for a long time. This story led me closer to God, who has become the steady and loving presence I never had. From that day forward, I promised myself that I would not let the pain of my past hold me back from the future I am building. I am choosing healing. I am choosing peace, and I am choosing to rise. I was 20 years old at this time.

## Partner relationship:

Another part of my story when I turned 25. I met someone that I thought God sent me. He was my everything. He was my first boyfriend. My goal as a christian was to wait and have sex after the marriage because I wanted to honor God and stay pure. He said he loved me and said he was a Christian. He told me that waiting until marriage wasn't something taught in the Bible. This was just a rule made up by people. Over time, I started to believe him. He kept saying we would get married soon, and I believed him.

After we had sex when I was 26, everything started to change. His attitude changed, and the way he spoke to me was different too. He began asking strange questions like, "If we are not together anymore, can we be friends?" I felt completely confused. I told him no. This was a sad moment of my life. I could not just be friends after everything I shared with him. I asked him for clarity. I asked him if I was still a priority to him. I had asked him to introduce me to his family. He introduced

INTRODUCTION

me to his sister. I asked him to speak to his parents, and he said he would, but he never told me if he actually did. I also asked him to talk to my sister, but he said he would not feel comfortable doing that. I felt upset, but I did not show it. At first, he talked about marrying me all the time. But after I spent one night with him, and had sex, I felt not okay at all. I asked him again about marriage, and he said, "Maybe soon, maybe next year... or maybe never." That hurt me deeply. He even started talking about one-night stands and said things like, "we are living in the 21st century," like it was normal. This really broke my heart. I told him I am not the kind of person who sleeps around. If I wanted to be with different people, I would have done that before I met him. I explained that I could not live like the world does. This is not who I am. This is when I started to realize he was not a true Christian. A true christian would not lead someone to sin. It felt like he was only with me because I was a virgin, not because he truly cared about me. I asked *God, why did I go through this? Why did I let him play with my feelings?*

After he started acting this way, I did not feel safe or at peace with him. I started to lose trust. Just two months after we had sex, he broke up with me. That hurt deeply, because I had wanted to stay pure for my future husband, but I did not. I was left heartbroken, confused, and full of regret. The way my ex-boyfriend talked and acted made me realize God was never really part of this relationship. There were signs I ignored because I was emotionally blinded, like how he kept pressuring me about marriage and always talked about sex. He was my first boyfriend, and he would often say things like, "You are so fresh and sexy," and that he wanted me to be his wife.

Before the breakup, I had prayed: *"God, if this man is not for me, please remove him."* And God did. After the relationship ended, I started to see everything more clearly. I also prayed and asked God to remove anyone from my life who was not meant to be there in my life and He did. God removed me from my mother and my sister. Our relationship was very unhealthy, but deep down, I still love them. When I was living with my mom, a family member warned me to stay away from her. They told me that my own mother said she wanted me to get into a car accident on the highway. They even said she wanted to put her hands on my neck. Hearing that was painful, but it showed me now that God was protecting me by moving me away from that situation. I asked God to forgive me, and to help heal my heart. I asked God I want to be close to Him more than ever, and He is. Little by little, God is restoring me. He is healing the broken pieces, and I am learning to trust Him more than ever before.

**Lessons Learned from the story:**

I always served God at a very young age around 9 years old. I had always tried to protect myself from that kind of pain and sin. I always did everything to respect myself. I always stay nice to people and always willing to help people around me. However, I never imagined that I could be weak in certain situations. My story taught people in my life can leave me, but God will always be there for me. I learned I should never trust man, but only God. **God is the Alpha and the Omega, the Beginning and the End.** He was there before anything existed, and He will still be there after everything else is gone. He sees the whole story of our lives from start to finish, and nothing is hidden from Him. Even when we feel lost, He already knows the way forward. He holds our past, present, and future in His hands. Through all the pain and struggles I have faced, through family

INTRODUCTION

hurt, broken relationships, and deep confusion, I can feel God calling me to something greater. I do not know what it is yet, but it feels big. Even though I do not have all the answers, I am choosing to trust Him. My future is in His hands. I believe He is writing a story bigger than I can imagine.

I hope my story helps you understand something very important: no matter what your past looks like, you can still choose to serve God. You can still walk in His purpose for your life just say Yes to God. I am saved by God. He gave me peace. I started to grow stronger and be closer to God. I began to understand who He created me to be.

If you read this book, I want you to know you are not alone. You do not have to be perfect. You just need to be willing. I believe when a woman says yes to God, everything starts to change. Hearts are healed. Faith grows. Families shift. Even generations can be impacted all because one woman said, "God, I am ready."

If you are holding this book, I believe this is your moment.

- Your time to trust.
- Your time to grow.
- Your time to say yes.

Let's walk this journey together and see what happens when we follow God with our whole hearts.

# 2

# Recognizing God's Call

Section 1: Understanding the Call of God

There comes a moment in every woman's life when she begins to feel a stirring, a quiet tug in her heart that whispers, *There is more.*
More than just getting by. More than keeping up. More than checking off boxes or following the crowd. That stirring deep inside you is often the first sign that God is calling you. But what does it really mean to be **called by God**?

What it means to be called by God? :

Being called by God does not always mean something big, flashy, or public. It does not mean you need to be holding a microphone or standing on a stage. It means that God has chosen you for something. Sometimes that "something" is raising Godly children. Sometimes it is starting a ministry, mentoring others, stepping out in faith at work, or simply drawing closer to Him.

## Biblical examples of women called by God:

Throughout the Bible, we see women just like you and me ordinary people who were called into extraordinary moments:

- **Esther**, a young woman who risked her life to save her people.
- **Mary**, a teenager called to carry the Savior of the world.
- **Deborah**, a judge and prophetess who led Israel to victory.
- **Ruth**, a widowed foreigner whose loyalty and faith placed her in the lineage of Jesus.

None of them started out knowing the whole plan. But they said yes..

## Common misconceptions about calling:

Sometimes we confuse God's calling with perfection or popularity. But calling does not mean you are always confident or ready. It does not mean you will be famous or applauded.

Here are a few common lies women believe about being called:

- "God only calls people who have it all together."
- "I am not spiritual enough for God to use me."
- "If it is hard or uncomfortable, it must not be God."

None of those things are true. In fact, God often chooses the ones who feel unqualified so that His strength can shine through their weakness.

## The difference between worldly ambition and divine assignment:

There is a big difference between chasing goals and following God.

**Worldly ambition** says: *"Make a name for yourself."*
**Divine assignment** says: *"Glorify God through your life."*

Ambition is not wrong but when it is not submitted to God, it can lead to burnout, comparison, and emptiness. A divine assignment, on the other hand, may look small on the outside, but it carries eternal impact.

**How God Speaks Today**

God is still speaking. The question is are we listening?

**Through Scripture**

God's Word is alive, and it is one of the most powerful ways He speaks. When you read the Bible, you are not just reading history you are hearing His heart. A single verse can give you direction, peace, or confirmation of what He's calling you to do.

**Through prayer and quiet time**

Sometimes, God speaks in stillness. He reveals His thoughts during prayer, worship, or quiet reflection. That gentle nudge in your heart? That unexpected idea or strong feeling of peace? It is often His voice.

**Through circumstances and other people**

God can use anything to speak, closed doors, unexpected opportunities, conversations, even challenges. He may speak through a mentor, a sermon, or something someone says that hits you deeply.

### The Inner Tug You Can't Ignore

*How to Recognize When God Is Calling You and What to Do Next*

Have you ever felt like something in your life was **off**, even though everything looked "fine" on the outside?

You go to work. You handle responsibilities. You smile. But deep down, you feel a quiet stirring. A nudge in your heart that says, *"There's more."*

That's the **inner tug**, and it's one of the ways God begins to call His daughters into something deeper.

It does not always come with a loud voice from Heaven or a dramatic sign. Most often, it starts with a **whisper** a holy restlessness you can't shake.

Here is how to recognize it, respond to it, and take action one faithful step at a time.

## 1. What Does the Inner Tug Feel Like?

It can feel like:

- A sudden or growing interest in a topic, group, or need
- A sense that God is asking more of you even if you do not know what
- Repeated thoughts, dreams, or conversations around the same subject
- Spiritual hunger like you want to go deeper, but do not know how
- A clear idea you can't stop thinking about, even if it scares you

## 2. Actionable Tips to Recognize the Tug

Keep a "God Tug" Journal

- Write down any repeated themes, dreams, scriptures, or conversations.
- Note when you feel most drawn to something or someone.
- Ask: *"What keeps coming up, even when I am not looking for it?"*

### Track Emotional Patterns

Ask yourself weekly:

- When do I feel drained or empty?
- When do I feel excited or alive?

- What gives me peace vs. what stirs anxiety? God often speaks through what stirs your spirit.

## Pay Attention to "Random" Confirmations

- Do certain verses, quotes, or messages keep appearing?
- Did someone say something that felt like it was meant for you?
- Do not brush off "coincidences" they are often confirmations.

3. How to Know It's From God (Not Just You)

It is normal to wonder if you are just imagining things. Here is how to test what you are feeling:

- Use the 3-Way Filter
- **Does it align with Scripture?** God will never call you to something that goes against His Word.
- **Does it draw you closer to Him?** If it brings you peace, purpose, or a deeper relationship with Him, it is likely from Him.
- **Does it serve others, not just you?** A God-calling always carries impact beyond yourself.
- Ask God Directly
- Pray: *"Lord, if this is from You, confirm it. If it is not, remove the desire."*
- Then listen. Give God space to answer through people, peace, or direction.

## 4. How to Respond to the Tug: Practical First Steps

You do not need to make a huge leap. Here is what you can do now:

**Start a Daily "Surrender" Moment**

- Each morning, say, "God, *I do not know where You are leading me, but I trust You. I am listening."*
- This simple prayer opens your heart to receive His guidance.

**Set Aside 10–15 Minutes of Stillness**

- Turn off your phone. Sit in silence with a notebook and pen.
- Ask God, "What *are You saying to me today?"*

- Write down anything that comes to mind: thoughts, pictures, words.

## Try the "Next 3 Steps" Exercise

Write these questions in your journal:

1. What is one small step I can take toward what I am sensing?
2. Who can I talk to for wise, Godly counsel?
3. What distractions or fears do I need to surrender?

## Find a Faith Partner

- Talk to a mentor, pastor, or spiritually grounded friend.
- Say, *"I feel like God is stirring something in me. Can we pray about it together?"*

**Do not walk through the tug alone; God often speaks through community:**

## Do not Dismiss the Tug Just Because It is Small

- God often starts with small steps: praying more consistently, writing a blog post, helping someone in need.
- Do not wait for the "big" moment. Say yes to the small one first.

## 5. Watch Out for Common Roadblocks

### ⚠ Fear
You think, "What *if I fail?*"

- Replace with: *"God never asked me to be perfect just to trust Him."*

### ⚠ Guilt

- You think, "I *have messed up too much."*

Truth: *God delights in using the broken and the willing.*

### ⚠ Comparison

- You think: *"She is already doing it better."*

*Reminder: God did not make a mistake when He called you. Your voice, your story, and your journey are unique.*

## 6. Confirming the Tug With God's Word

When the tug is strong, anchor it in scripture. Here are some verses to pray and reflect on:

- **Isaiah 30:21** – *"Your ears shall hear a word behind you, saying, 'This is the way, walk in it.'"*
- **Jeremiah 29:11–13**—"You "will *seek Me and find Me when you seek Me with all your heart."*
- **Proverbs 3:5–6** – *"Trust in the Lord with all your heart... He*

*will direct your paths."*
- **Philippians 2:13** – *"For it is God who works in you to will and to act in order to fulfill His good purpose."*

**Tip:** Write one of these verses on a sticky note and put it on your mirror, dashboard, or journal as a daily reminder.

## 7. Reflection Questions (To Help You Go Deeper)

- What part of my life feels "too small" that God may actually want to use?
- When do I feel closest to God and how can I make more space for that?
- What is one thing I need to surrender to take a next step?
- What would I do for God if I was not afraid?
- What has God been showing me lately, either about Himself or about me
- What spiritual battle are you currently fighting now that others might not see
- When was the last time you really felt the presence of God? What was happening?

## Final Encouragement

That gentle tug you feel? It is not your imagination.
It is God saying, *"Daughter, I have more for you."*
You do not need to understand everything to move forward.
You just need to be willing to say yes.
Not to a title.
Not to a platform.

But to a **relationship** to a daily walk with the One who loves you more than you could ever know.

**Let the tug move you. Let the yes free you. Let the journey begin.**

**Signs that you are being called to more**

- You feel restless or unfulfilled in your current season.
- You sense God stirring something in your heart.
- You feel drawn to something outside your comfort zone.

**Emotional and spiritual restlessness**

Sometimes you will feel emotional tension like something is not right or is missing. You may even feel spiritually dry, not because God has left, but because He is calling you deeper.

**Distinguishing between fear and conviction**

Fear tells you to run.

Conviction tells you to move forward.

One paralyzes you. The other pulls you closer to God.

Learn to ask: *Am I afraid, or is God gently challenging me to grow?*

**Section 2: Identifying Your Starting Point**

Before you start following God's call, you need to know where you are right now. You can't move forward without understanding where you are starting from.

**Are you stagnant, confused, or drifting?**

Assessing your current spiritual condition

Ask yourself honestly:

- Am I **stagnant**—not growing, just coasting?
- Am I **confused**—unsure of where God wants me?

- Am I **drifting**—going through the motions but feeling disconnected?

**Are you distracted or spiritually hungry?**
Or maybe you are distracted. Maybe you are spiritually hungry but do not know where to start.

**Journaling and reflecting honestly**
Start by journaling. Reflect on what you are feeling. Be honest with God. He already knows your heart

Barriers that Hinder Clarity

Fear of failure or inadequacy

"I am not good enough."

"What if I mess it up?"

These are lies the enemy uses to keep you stuck. God does not ask for perfection. He asks for your heart.

**Comparing yourself to others**
God did not call you to live someone else's story. He called you to live your own. Stop measuring your purpose by someone else's progress.

**Past wounds or guilt**

- Sometimes, it is the pain we have not dealt with that blocks us from hearing God clearly. Let Him into those broken places. He is not ashamed of them. He wants to heal them.
- Listening Before Leaping
- God often invites us into stillness before sending us into action.

**Why God calls you into stillness first**
Stillness teaches trust. It deepens your faith. It clears away the noise so you can hear His voice. Do not rush through this

part it is where the roots grow deep.

**Developing discernment**

Discernment is the ability to sense what is from God and what is not. It grows over time, through prayer, Scripture, and experience. Ask God for wisdom and then pay attention to how He answers.

**What to do while you wait**

1. Waiting is not wasting.
2. Serve where you are.
3. Pray regularly.
4. Stay close to God.
5. Be faithful in the small things. God is watching your heart, not just your actions.

Section 3: Saying Yes to the Process

Surrender does not happen all at once. It is a daily choice. A process. But it is also the most freeing decision you will ever make.

**The Power of Surrender:**

**Trusting God more than your plans**

You may have your own ideas about how life should go but when you surrender to God, you say, "I trust Your plan more than mine."

**Giving up control to gain peace**

Control brings stress. Surrender brings peace. When you let go, God steps in and does what you never could on your own.

**What surrender looks like in everyday life**

1. It is saying "yes" even when you are scared.

2. It is following through even when it is uncomfortable.

3. It is choosing obedience when no one is watching.

**Faith vs. Feelings:**

**Why your feelings are not always facts**

Feelings are real, but they do not always tell the truth. God's Word is your foundation not your emotions.

**Walking by faith even in doubt**

You don't need perfect faith to obey. You just need enough faith to take the next step.

**Grounding yourself in God's Word.**

God's Word keeps you steady. It reminds you of who you are, what you are called to, and who is walking with you.

Your Yes Changes Everything

**Breaking the cycle of delay**

You do not have to keep waiting for the perfect moment. Start now with whatever you have, right where you are

**The ripple effect of obedience**

Your yes won't just impact your life. It will impact your family. Your community. Maybe even generations to come.

**Preparing for spiritual growth**

God is always working. As you keep saying yes, He will keep growing you. You will look back one day and be amazed at how far He has brought you.

Are you ready to say yes?

It does not have to be perfect.

It just has to be real.

This is the beginning of something beautiful.

# 3

# Becoming Rooted—Laying a Spiritual Foundation

A tree can't grow tall and strong unless its roots go deep. The same is true for you.

If you want to walk boldly in your calling and stay steady when life gets hard, you need more than motivation. You need a solid foundation built on your relationship with God.

In this chapter, we will explore how to move beyond surface-level faith, heal from what is been holding you back, and surround yourself with people who help you grow not pull you away.

*Let's dig into the roots.*

*Section 1: Building a Real Relationship with God*

A calling from God can't be sustained by weekend faith. To fully surrender and walk in your purpose, you must know the One who called you, not just know *about* Him.

**Going Beyond Religion**

Many people grow up with religion, rules, routines, and rituals but still feel disconnected from God. Why? Because religion without relationship leads to burnout and emptiness.

**Relationship vs. routine**

- Going to church is good, but it is not enough.
- Checking off devotionals does not mean you have met with God.

Ask: *Do I know about God, or do I know His heart?*

### Knowing God's heart

- God is not distant. He wants to reveal His heart to you.
- Get curious: *What brings God joy? What breaks His heart?*
- The more you know Him, the more you trust Him.

### Intimacy through vulnerability

- Be honest with God. Tell Him when you are confused, frustrated, or scared.
- He does not want a performance. He wants your **presence**.

### Practical Tip:

- Write a "Dear God" letter once a week. Don't filter it. Just be real. Then read Scripture and let Him speak back to you through His Word.

### Cultivating Consistent Prayer Life

Prayer is more than a spiritual task; it is a daily conversation with your Creator. But consistency takes intersectionality.

**Making time, not excuses**

- Do not wait until you "feel spiritual." Start with 5–10 minutes a day.
- Build prayer into natural rhythms: during your commute, walks, or while doing chores.

**How to pray without feeling fake**

- Be simple and honest. God values sincerity over fancy words.
- Try this prayer format: **Thank You, Help Me, Teach Me, Show Me.**

**Listening in prayer, not just talking**

- Don't rush through your words and move on.
- After praying, sit still for a few moments and simply listen.
- Ask, "God, *what are You saying to me today?*"

*Practical Tip:*

- *Set a timer for 5 minutes of silence after prayer. Keep a notebook nearby to write down any thoughts or impressions you receive.*

**Feeding Your Faith**
You can't grow spiritually if you are spiritually starving.
Faith is strengthened through the Word of God.
**Daily Bible reading habits**

- Choose a specific time daily (morning or evening).
- Start with a short, manageable plan (like the Gospels or Psalms).

**Studying vs. skimming Scripture**

- Don't rush. Ask: *What is God saying here? How does this apply to me?*
- Use tools like study Bibles or devotionals to go deeper.

**Applying the Word to your life**
Scripture is not just to read. It's to live.
Example: If you read about forgiveness, ask yourself who you need to forgive today.
**Practical Tip:**
Pick one verse a day and write it on a sticky note or in your phone. Reflect on it throughout the day and apply it to real situations.

## Section 2: Healing to Move Forward

You can't run freely if you are still tied to past pain.
To walk confidently in your calling, you need to be **whole**, not just busy.

**Releasing What Is Holding You Back:**
**Unforgiveness and emotional baggage**

- Who do you need to forgive—others, yourself, or even God?
- Holding onto hurt blocks your spiritual hearing.

### Releasing the past to embrace the future

- You can't move forward if your heart is still in yesterday.
- Ask God to help you let go of what you keep replaying.

### Deliverance from hidden strongholds

- These may be lies you believe: *"I am not worthy." "I will always be broken."*
- Ask the Holy Spirit to break strongholds and replace lies with truth.

### Practical Tip:

Write down what you need to release. Pray over it. Then tear it up or burn it safely as a symbolic act of surrender

### Inner Healing Through Christ

Healing is a process, and God walks with you through every step.

### Allowing God to address your wounds

Invite Him into your pain, your memories, your disappointments.

Ask, "Jesus, *where were You in that moment?*" Let Him reveal truth.

### Seeking counseling or mentorship if needed

- Healing is not a sign of weakness. It is a sign of strength.
- Do not be afraid to seek help from a Christian counselor or mentor.

### Rewriting your story with truth

- You are not your past. You are not your pain.
- Let God show you who you really are and rewrite your story in truth.

**Practical Tip:**
Speak this out loud daily: *"I am who God says I am. I am not my past. I am walking in healing."*
Learning to Love Yourself as God Does
It is hard to believe you are called if you secretly believe you are not worthy.

### Reclaiming your identity in Christ

- You are chosen, loved, forgiven, and called.
- Ephesians 2:10 says you are *God's masterpiece*.

### From shame to self-worth

- Shame says, *"I am not enough."*
- God says, *"You are more than enough because I am in you."*

### Speaking life over yourself

- Life and death are in the power of your tongue (Proverbs 18:21).
- Declare truth even when you do not feel it. Your words shape your mindset.

**Practical Tip:**

Create 3 "I am" declarations based on Scripture. Say them aloud every morning.
Examples:

- *"I am loved by God."*
- *"I am strong in the Lord."*
- *"I am chosen for a purpose."*

Section 3: Surrounding Yourself with the Right People
You become like the people you spend time with.

If you want to grow spiritually, you must protect your environment.

The Power of Godly Community
**Why you can't do this alone**

- God designed us to grow through connection.
- Lone-wolf faith leads to isolation and burnout

**Finding or building sisterhood**

- Look for small groups, Bible studies, or church communities.
- If you can't find one, start one. Invite two or three friends to pray or read with you weekly.

**The role of spiritual accountability**

- A true friend does not just cheer you on. They call you higher.
- Accountability keeps you on track with your goals and your

growth.

**Practical Tip:**
Text a friend today: *"Let's pray together this week or check in spiritually. I need a growth partner."*
**Mentorship and Discipleship:**
**Identifying spiritual mentors**

- Look for someone who lives out their faith consistently.
- Do not focus on perfection: look for humility and wisdom.

**Being teachable and humble**

- Ask questions. Be open to correction.
- Growth happens when you are willing to listen and learn.

**Learning from others' testimonies**

- Ask people how God brought them through hard times.
- Testimonies remind you that if God did it for them, He can do it for you.

**Practical Tip:**
Ask one person this week: *"Can I learn from your faith journey?"* Set a coffee or phone date.
**Letting Go of Toxic Ties:**
**Recognizing Unequally Yoked Relationships**

- Do your close relationships pull you toward God or away from Him?
- You can love people without letting them lead your life.

## Boundaries and grace

- Boundaries are not rejection. They are protection.
- Set clear limits on who has access to your heart and energy.

## Making room for divine connections

- Sometimes, God has to close doors before He opens new ones.
- Trust that when you let go of the wrong people, He will bring the right ones.

**Practical Tip:**
Write down 3 people who speak life into you and 3 who drain your peace. Begin setting healthy boundaries where needed

## Final Encouragement: You are Growing Roots

You do not have to be perfect to grow just planted.

This season is not wasted. Every moment spent in prayer, healing, study, or relationship-building is preparing you to stand strong in your calling.

Stay rooted.

Stay real.

And let God build your foundation one layer at a time.

# 4

# Walking in Purpose—Discovering and Using Your Gifts

Saying "yes" to God is the beginning. But walking in purpose is where that yes becomes real.

M any women ask:
"What am I really called to do?"
"How can I use what I have for God's glory?"
"Am I even gifted at all?"
The truth is: you are.

God did not create you to live on autopilot. He gave you specific gifts, strengths, and passions so that you can reflect His love in a way only *you* can.

This chapter will help you identify those gifts, trust God through the unknown, and step forward boldly and obediently.

## Section 1: Identifying Your God-Given Gifts

Every believer has spiritual gifts, and when you discover and use them, you come alive in a new way.

**Gifts of the Spirit vs. Natural Talents:**
**What are spiritual gifts?**

Spiritual gifts are special abilities given by the Holy Spirit to help build the church and serve others. They include things like:

- Teaching, wisdom, encouragement, faith, leadership, hospitality, discernment, and more (see Romans 12, 1 Corinthians 12, Ephesians 4).

They are different from talents like singing, painting, or organizing, but God can use both.

**How to uncover yours through prayer and Scripture**

- Ask God, "What *have You placed inside of me?*"
- Read about spiritual gifts in Scripture and ask the Holy Spirit to highlight which ones resonate.
- Look for fruit; where does your impact seem to grow naturally?

**Understanding where God uses your abilities**

- God often uses our gifts where people are hurting, overlooked, or hungry for truth.
- Example: If you are always drawn to encourage hurting people, that is not random; it is a clue.

# WALKING IN PURPOSE—DISCOVERING AND USING YOUR GIFTS

**Tip:** Keep a list of moments when you feel most "alive" or energized while helping others. There's purpose in that.

### Strengths and Passion Alignment:
### What brings you joy and burdens your heart?

- Joy and burden often point to calling.
- What injustice breaks your heart? What topic could you talk about for hours?
- That is likely where God wants to use you.

### Recognizing recurring themes in your life

- Are you always leading, even when you do not mean to?
- Do people naturally come to you for advice, comfort, or organization?

### Your patterns reveal purpose:
### Confirmations through people and open doors

- Has someone ever said, *"You are gifted in this"*?
- Has God opened doors in areas you did not even seek out?
- These moments are often divine hints.

**Tip:** Ask 2–3 trusted people, *"What gifts do you see in me?"* You might be surprised at the answers.

### Tools for Discovery:
### Spiritual gifts assessments

- Take a trusted online or church-based assessment.
- Use it as a starting point, not a final answer.

- Reflect on the results in prayer.

**Journaling insights and prayer revelations**

- After you serve or help someone, journal how it felt and what impact it had.
- Ask God during prayer, *"What did You make me for?"*

**Talking to mentors or pastors**

- They may see things you do not.
- Ask them where they see your fruit and growth.

**Tip:** Combine prayer + people + action to get a clearer picture of your purpose.

## Section 2: Trusting God with the Unknown

You might not have it all figured out—but that's okay.

God rarely shows the full picture at once. He calls you to **walk by faith**, not by sight.

**Walking Without a Blueprint:**
**Why clarity comes in steps**

- God often reveals the *next step,* not the whole staircase.
- Obedience in one season unlocks direction for the next.

**Trusting without knowing the full picture**

- Abraham followed God "not knowing where he was going" (Hebrews 11:8).
- Let go of the need to know everything and choose to know *Him* deeply.

**Taking the first step of faith**

- Start where you are with what you have.
- God can't multiply what you do not move.

**Tip:** Set a goal to take *one obedient action* this week, whether it is joining a group, serving, or sending an email you have been avoiding.

**Overcoming Imposter Syndrome:**
**"Why me?" and "I am not enough" lies**

- These thoughts often come when you are close to breakthrough.

- 
- Remember: God does not call the qualified. He qualifies the call.

**Affirming your call through truth**
Speak these over yourself:

- *"God chose me, and He is with me."*
- *"My weakness makes room for His strength."*
- *"I am equipped through Christ."*

**Replacing insecurity with God-confidence**
Confidence is not about being sure of yourself. It is about being sure of *Him*.

Let your courage come from His presence, not your resume.

**Tip:** Make a list of God's promises that silence your doubts. Keep it visible.

**Embracing the Process:**
**God prepares you before He sends you**

- Before David became king, he learned courage with sheep and slingshots.
- Every job, heartbreak, delay, or shift is part of your preparation.

**Seasons of pruning and planting**

- Some seasons feel slow or even painful, but they are meant to grow your roots.
- Let God remove what is holding you back so He can grow

what is meant to stay.

**Patience in spiritual development**

- Do not rush the process. Growth takes time.
- Stay faithful in small things. God sees everything.

**Tip:** Write a timeline of your spiritual journey. Look at how far God has already brought you.
Section 3: Taking Bold Action
Once you discover your gifts, the next step is to use them. Not perfectly. Not all at once. But **boldly and faithfully**.
Faith Requires Movement
**Doing it scared and still obedient**
Courage is not the absence of fear. It is obedience in the face of fear.

Start messy. God honors motion.
**Small steps matter**
One conversation. One prayer. One post. One yes.

**Obedience adds up:**

**Obedience over perfection**

- God never asked you to be perfect just to say yes.
- He will handle the results. Your job is to show up.

**Tip:** Write this down and keep it close: *"Start small. Start scared. Start anyway."*
**Becoming a Vessel of Influence**

1. Serving with your gifts
2. Leading without needing a title

- You do not need a mic to make a difference.
- Influence is about impact, not position.

**Being a light in your circle of influence**

- Your workplace, family, school, or online platform is your mission field.
- Let your character speak louder than your words.

**Tip:** Ask God each morning, *"Who can I serve today using what You have given me?"*
Staying Rooted in Purpose

**How to avoid burnout**
Stay connected to the Source (John 15:5).
Do not serve for applause. Serve from overflow.
**Regular check-ins with God**
Ask often: *"God, am I still aligned with You?"*
Let Him redirect you when needed.
**Resting and resetting with Him**
Even Jesus rested. So should you.
Sabbath is not optional. It is vital.
Tip: Schedule regular times for rest, reflection, and worship. Your purpose is stronger when your soul is refreshed.
Final Encouragement: You Were Made For This
You do not have to have all the answers.
You do not need the perfect plan.
You just need to know the One who gave you your gifts and

trust Him enough to use them.

God did not create you to blend in.

He created you to shine, to serve, and to make a difference right where you are.

So ask yourself:

- What has God already placed in my hands?
- What is my next small step of obedience?

Then do it.

Not for applause. Not for perfection.

But because your obedience is worship and your gifts are a reflection of His glory.

# 5

## A woman of God does not just say "yes" once; she lives a lifestyle of surrender.

She seeks God's presence daily, not just His promises. She becomes the kind of woman who does not chase purpose for applause but lives from the overflow of knowing who she is and whose she is.

This chapter will help you shift from doing for God to becoming with God living in step with Him through daily disciplines, Spirit-led choices, and a life that influences others for eternity.

*Section 1: Character Over Calling*

Many women are eager to know their calling, but God is first concerned with who we are becoming, not what we are doing.

**God cares more about who you're growing into than what you do:**

**Holy Spirit qualities**

In Galatians 5:22–23, we are reminded of the evidence of

a life led by the Holy Spirit: qualities like love, joy, peace, patience, kindness, goodness, faithfulness, gentleness, and self-control. These traits should be visible in our everyday actions and character.

A Spirit-filled woman does not just do ministry; she reflects God's nature in how she speaks, loves, and lives.

**Maturity through testing and trials**

- Trials do not disqualify you; they *develop* you.
- God uses hard seasons to build endurance, resilience, and wisdom.

**Building integrity and humility**

- Private obedience matters more than public success.
- Be the same woman in secret as you are in public.

**Practical Tip:** Do a weekly "fruit check." Ask: *"Did I reflect patience? Kindness? Self-control this week?"* Do not beat yourself up; just grow

**Daily Spiritual Disciplines**

Discipline leads to depth. Not out of guilt, but out of love.

**Morning routines with God**

- Start your day in God's presence before the world's pressure.
- Try this: Worship for 5 minutes, read Scripture for 10 minutes, and pray for 5 minutes.

**Fasting, journalism, and worship**

- Fasting breaks strongholds and helps you hear clearly.
- Journalism helps you track growth and listen to God's whispers.
- Worship shifts your atmosphere and aligns your heart.

**Staying alert in the spiritual realm**

- Do not live unaware; spiritual warfare is real.
- Guard your mind, watch your influences, and cover your day in prayer.

**Practical Tip:** Schedule "soul check" days, short times to fast from distractions (like social media) and tune in to God.

**Living Like Jesus**

Jesus was bold but also tender. He confronted and comforted. He led with love and truth.

**Servant leadership**

Greatness in the Kingdom looks like humility and service. Ask, "How *can I help someone today?*"

**Radical compassion and grace**

- See people through God's eyes, not just your perspective.

**Reflecting Christ in word and deed**

- Speak life, act in love, and walk in peace.
- You may be the only "Bible" someone reads today.

**Practical Tip:** Before entering any space (home, school, or work), ask, "God, *how can I represent You here?*"

## Section 2: Being Led by the Spirit

A surrendered woman does not chase every opportunity; she listens for direction.
She is led by the **Spirit**, not driven by pressure.
**Living in Alignment with God's Voice:**
**Developing spiritual sensitivity**

- Spend time in silence and solitude. Practice listening.
- Ask God to help you recognize His voice in everyday moments.

**Prompted vs. pressured living**

- God's guidance brings peace, not panic.
- Learn to distinguish between what feels urgent vs. what's divinely timed.

**Saying no to good things for the God things**

- Not every good opportunity is a *God* opportunity.
- Protect your "yes" so it stays powerful and intentional.

**Practical Tip:** Before you commit to anything new, ask, *"God, is this from You, or just something that looks good?"*

**Discernment in Decision-Making**

Discernment helps you know *when*, *how*, and *if* to move forward.
**Filters for spiritual choices**

- Does this align with God's Word?
- Will this glorify God or glorify me?
- Does it produce peace or confusion?

**Surrendered yes vs. obligated yes**

- A surrendered yes is offered with joy and peace.
- An obligated yes is often rooted in guilt, fear, or pressure.

**Trusting God with closed doors**

- If God closes a door, it is for protection, not punishment.
- Delay does not mean denial.

A WOMAN OF GOD DOES NOT JUST SAY "YES" ONCE; SHE LIVES A...

**Practical Tip:** Keep a "Discernment Journal" to write out decisions, seek God's guidance, and track His direction.

### · Obedience as a Lifestyle

Obedience is not a one-time event; it's a rhythm.

**Why obedience is not a one-time thing**

- Every day, God invites you to trust Him, sometimes in big ways, often in small ones.

**Staying faithful in the mundane**

- Washing dishes, going to work, showing up on time: it's all worship when done with the right heart.
- Faithfulness in the small prepares you for the big.

**Fruitfulness through surrender**

- Surrender leads to lasting fruit, not just fast results.
- God grows you through what you give Him daily.

**Practical Tip:** Ask yourself each morning, "What *does obedience look like for me today?*" Then do it, even if it is simple.

## Section 3: Empowering Others Through Your Journey'

Your growth is not just for you—it's for those watching you.
Your obedience becomes someone else's inspiration.
· Your Story Matters
**Testimony as a weapon and encouragement**
Revelation 12:11 says we overcome "by the blood of the Lamb and the word of our testimony."

Your story breaks chains for others.

### How your obedience inspires others
Someone is waiting to hear how God brought you through.

Even your quiet "yes" encourages someone else to trust God more.

### Sharing your walk authentically

- You do not have to share from a place of perfection, just honesty.
- Your "I am still growing" testimony is just as powerful as your "I made it" one.

**Practical Tip:** Write out your story in 3 short parts: *before Jesus, how He met you, and where He's leading you now.* Practice sharing it with love and confidence.

Mentoring and Disciplining Other Women

### Becoming a guide, not a guru

- You are not leading from above; you're walking alongside.

Point women to *God*, not yourself.

### Multiplying what God has done in you

- As God grows you, pour that into someone else.
- You do not need a degree to disciple; you just need a willing heart.

### Raising up the next generation of surrendered women

- Look for young women to encourage, listen to, and pray

for.
- You are not just making disciples; you are building a legacy.

**Practical Tip:** Ask God to highlight one woman to walk with this season. Start with coffee and conversation.
  · Living a Legacy of Faith

**Impact beyond your lifetime**

- Your prayers, obedience, and love echo beyond what you can see.
- A surrendered life touches generations.
- Break chains from your family's past.
- Leave a spiritual legacy for your children, nieces, or sisters in Christ.

**Spiritual inheritance and generational blessings: Finishing well, not just starting strong**

- Faithfulness until the end matters.
- Your strength does not come from hustle; it comes from hope.

**Practical Tip:** Write a "legacy letter," a prayer or message you would want your daughter, mentee, or future readers to hear about your walk with God.
You do not become a woman of God overnight.
It is a daily choice. A daily surrender. A daily yes.
You may not feel "ready," but God is not asking for perfection; He's asking for your **willingness**.

Stay rooted in character.
Stay close to His Spirit.
Stay focused on others.
And know that **your surrendered life** is planting seeds of eternal impact.

## Conclusion: Your Yes Is Just the Beginning

As you come to the end of this book, take a deep breath and look back at how far you have come.

## Recap of the Journey

Throughout these chapters, we have walked together from uncertainty to clarity—point A to point B:

· In **Chapter 1**, you discovered what it means to recognize God's call and identify the tug He placed on your heart. You were invited to say yes to the journey, even if you did not know all the steps.

· In **Chapter 2**, you laid the foundation of a deep relationship with God. You learned the importance of spiritual disciplines, inner healing, and surrounding yourself with the right community.

· In **Chapter 3**, you began exploring your unique gifts and callings. You embraced boldness, faith, and obedience, learning that walking in purpose is not about perfection but daily surrender.

In **Chapter 4**, you matured into a woman of God who is not only walking in purpose but helping others rise as well. You learned how to live a life led by the Spirit and build a legacy that glorifies God.

## Final Words of Encouragement

If you have made it this far, it means you are not just curious; you are committed. You have made the decision to fully surrender and follow God's calling on your life. And I want to remind you: **God does not call the qualified; He qualifies the called.**

You do not have to know everything. You do not have to have it all together.

You just have to say yes. Again and again. Every day.

When women say yes to God, families change. Communities change. Generations change.

Let your life be proof that full surrender is the most powerful, fulfilling, and freeing decision a woman can ever make.

·

# 6

# One Last Request: Share Your Yes

If this book encouraged, empowered, or equipped you in any way, I would be so grateful if you would take a moment to leave a review. Your words could be the confirmation another woman is waiting for the sign she needs to begin her own journey of surrender.

May God bless you as you walk forward with courage, purpose, and a heart fully surrendered to Him.

**You've said yes. Now watch what God will do.**

If you enjoy the book, it would mean a lot for me if you can leave a review on Amazon. I would love to hear from you

If you need additional information or want to learn about me, you can find me at

Youtube Link: https://www.youtube.com/@JourneyToGrowth9

Instagram Link: https://www.instagram.com/journeytogrowth9/

Or

https://www.instagram.com/judicaelle_celestin/

Facebook: https://www.facebook.com/judicaelle.celestin/

God bless you! Thank you for reading.
Judicaelle Celestin

Resource:

Celestin, Judicaelle. *What Happens When Women Fully Surrender and Follow God's Calling?* 2025.

www.ingramcontent.com/pod-product-compliance
Lightning Source LLC
LaVergne TN
LVHW012251070526
838201LV00108B/320/J